BRO

BROKEN FACE

ZUZU ALEXI CUPIDO

PARTRIDGE
A Penguin Random House Company

To order additional copies of this book, contact
Toll Free 0800 990 914 (South Africa)
+44 20 3014 3997 (outside South Africa)
orders.africa@partridgepublishing.com

www.partridgepublishing.com/africa

Note from the author:

I wrote this book with the purpose to report, to explain, and mostly to persuade. I have tried my utmost best not to distort facts in order to support a point of view and therefore I am presenting the facts as truthfully as I can. I tried my best to be accurate to describe the story to bring the reader to the reality of the subject. What I wrote in this book is not fiction but true events.

It is true that some people would say that this is not the worst-case scenario and I agree 100 per cent, but I have seen with my eyes the emotional pain and hardship that had shaped this woman into fighting to restore her name and her innocence. Her situation made her break a silence that was present in many people's lives but they simply walked away from it all – powerless to fight back for justice to take its course. Some never recovered from what had happened to them; others took their lives because they were betrayed by a system they stood no chance to stand up to. Many are still broke and jobless without hope or any future left for them. Sandra decided to break the silence of an injustice that was time and again taking place to those whose democratic rights were undermined. Her trigger words to me was 'I will not walk away without a fight. I will fight back to restore my name because one is innocent until proven guilty. I will in no uncertain terms prove my innocence because that is what I am – innocent. I am not fighting with the Corporate Z. I am fighting for my name.'

After hearing these words, what else could I do but to rest my case? I was inspired by Sandra's bravery and that made me write her story. Through this journey I have learnt so much and have known from her experience that no one should ever underestimate the perseverance of a single mother. Her story brought the best out of me and has taught me that life is a war we fight for the sake of survival. It is a fact that the human race is in the race for survival.

Case Scenario:

For twenty-one years Sandra worked hard in the Corporate Z starting as a sorter and working her way up to post master. I am sure that you will agree with me that it was hard work, right? The pages of this book will take you through the emotions and hardships she endured but the day she was dismissed with an unfounded charge she vowed to herself that she would not be a victim. She prepared herself for the worse but still believing in her innocence knowing that evil never slumbers. The handwriting was on the wall and the burning flame of courage was burning bright within her soul, therefore she took her case to CCMA and later it ended up in the Labour Court. Anyway, with an invincible determination believing that she will overcome every obstacle, she succeeded against the odds.

I thank Sandra for trusting me and giving me the opportunity to write her story. This book, *Broken Face*, is dedicated to all the victims who were destroyed but not defeated and who waited for the one who would take action. Sandra, I believe, was the person to take action. The victims are now the winners who were in a losing game but now their attitudes have become more important to them than the tragedies of the past. They are slowly making peace with their anger. They are becoming victorious over their losses. Sandra believes that all victims are surely overcoming their sorrows and are starting to live again.

Broken Face is a book to help the victims who were manhandled to overcome. We hope that this book can help them to regain their strength and to rise up and be healed. We cannot change the past but we cannot allow the past to determine the future any longer. This book has nothing to do with revenge but it is about taking back one's self-worth. This book is about facts and Sandra and I made every attempt to put the facts together without exaggeration. During the preparation to put the book together a lot of emotions were released. These emotions and tears during her interviews helped Sandra to rid herself from the hatred she had developed. She was adamant not to remain under subjection of a defect of justice, despite the fear that the news will spread like a virus and that she will be looked at with judgmental gazes and fall victim to the slandering tongues of society. Not only was it imperative for her to stand up and fight – it was her democratic right as a citizen. The willingness within took root and her mind was made up for the challenge.

We trust that all victims would realize that now is the time for them to be free from the past and to forgive and forget. This is the time and the place; Sandra is the person, and I wrote this book for you and I quote, 'If their deeds did not kill you then you are still breathing but for those who died we will always remember why.'

Zuzu Alexi Cupido

Broken Face is a true story from the Republic of South Africa.

Acknowledgments:

My professional team — *Black Business Journal*'s Nomhle Mnube and Xolani Martin for trusting me to walk this mile.

My proofreaders — My two daughters, Tribal Ludi Cupido and Zasha Moonchild Cupido, for the many nights they had to offer up to help bring the final touches to perfection. Also Siyabonga Maxwell Thusini for his role and input.

I hereby also thank Al Mallorca, senior publishing consultant at Partridge Publishing for her patience and trust in me.

My designer — Tshego Nyatlo for working overtime on such a brilliant design for the book cover.

My manager — My husband and business partner, Everitte Cupido, who is my motivator, my guide, and the very crutch I lean on.

Sandra and family — Thank you for trusting me with your story. Your pain was my pain too and I have learnt some life skills from your ordeal.

Quote: 'Never underestimate the perseverance of a single mother.'

Zuzu Alexi Cupido

PROLOGUE

Our neighbours laugh at me when they see me. The reason is that they cannot believe I turned out to be such a different person. They all remember me as the girl with the antics. Aunt Winnie saw me the other day and broke into a childish laughter saying mockingly, 'Oh, Babsie's child, you were such a blooming naughty girl, I cannot believe that you turned out to be such a responsible mother. Look at you.' The old lady from my neighbourhood was saying that with such animation.

'Was I really that naughty, Aunt Winnie?' I asked jokingly.

'Oh! And how. I remember the way you were teasing Daisy saying she owns the local zoo.'

Granny Daisy was the shebeen queen who lived on the corner next to us. She had three dogs, a goat, a sheep, a duck, and a hen she called Peter but would pronounce it as Pietà. When Granny Daisy walked to the shop, her animals would walk with her but the funny side of it was they all walked in a row behind her, and Peter sat on her shoulder. It was a humorous sight for us children and we would laugh. I was the one shouting, 'Left, right, left, right, forward march,' and the other kids would mimic the way I marched saying 'There goes the farmyard bodyguards!'

Granny Daisy called us ridiculous ignorant snotheads that knew nothing about farm life. She was from the Transkei and had travelled from there with her animals to come live in the city. However, she always picked on me and would instruct Peter to charge at me. When Peter charged he would jump on your shoulder and grab your hair and pull. Not a very nice experience – I had a few of those. However, Granny Daisy liked me and would on certain occasions ask me to scrub her kitchen floor for fifty cents and three toffies. Years later she took all her animals and moved back to the farm in Transkei, telling everyone she was fed up with the city life and leaving it.

By the way, that was how I obtained my spending money during school breaks when we didn't go to Kimberley to visit my grandmother. I washed dishes for Aunty Rose and Aunt Fila and Linda. Linda was that kind of girl whose *milkshake* brought all the boys to the yard. But as for housecleaning, well, it was not her forte. Linda's fame with the boys did not allow her to do housework the way she should while her parents were at work. Therefore Linda would call me out to help, but their house was hectic. Linda had five very untidy brothers and she was the only girl in the family. Linda was twelve years older than me. She would play netball with her friends or hang around with the boys who liked her. As a result she neglected her chores, but to escape from a hiding she would call me to help. I did not mind because Linda was a good paying client. It was never a problem to pay me R1,00 and in those days a rand was a brown note and one could buy a lot with it. It was an honour for a child to have it. Having a rand in my hands made me always feel important. It was nice helping her because after cleaning she would paint my fingernails with natural nail polish and would tell me if I get to her age I must always look good.

There were just those days when I was not in the mood for other people's dirty houses. I had one of those days with Linda. I offered to help out but the minute I walked into that kitchen my offer became my nightmare. The kitchen table was covered in breadcrumbs from one end to the other. There were dirty coffee mugs and the knives were covered with peanut butter and jam. The sugar ants had found their way to have a feast. Anyone who took a look at that scene would get heart palpitations immediately. As for my heart it stood dead still, too scared to pump blood. The skin on my cheeks was stiffening up and my head made a forty-five degree spin. As for the dishrags, wow! Those dishrags . . . Never mind. With a kitchen like the one I was looking at now, standing in total shock made my knees weak. My mouth stood open as if I paused on a yawn. If I did not manage to close my mouth in time my jaws were going to be locked.

One did not know where to start, and in those days there were no teabags; we used tea leaves in a teapot and those leaves could not go down the kitchen sink because the drain would get blocked. Some of the leaves were spilled all over the floor, but the teapot with the tea leaves – that would be my passport out of here. I looked at the kitchen in total disgust and I realized that this whole house was in a state of emergency. The only way to fix the problem was to break the house down and rebuild it from scratch. As for lazy Linda and her brothers, they needed to be arrested for *household* indecency.

Besides the dirty mugs on the kitchen table, the sink was stacked with unwashed dishes. My heart was beating and I looked at Linda and asked her, 'Will you at least dry them if I wash up?'

'No, man puppet, gee! I am going to make up all the beds.' Her answer was not what I wanted to hear, and in my mind I started to really work on a way of escape. It was the only way because now I was feeling like an illegal alien on a foreign planet. My eyes went back to the ants that were still in the line of duty and I couldn't help but wonder why didn't Linda observe them and get wise. Did she want to remain a sluggard for the rest of her life?

'Okay, go make the beds, and I will start by getting rid of that tea leaves,' I calmly instructed Linda; with eagerness Linda adhered, showing great appreciation for the help but not knowing what I was planning. As a child I liked to be loyal but to show loyalty now was a bit complicated. I just didn't have the steam for all the dishes now with pots and pans, hell, no – it was time to run. Those dishes were piled up from last night and already carried a foul odour.

When Linda was out of sight, I disappeared through the kitchen door with the teapot, pretending that I was about to empty the leaves in the dirt bin. I looked around and remembered that the gate made a screeching noise and that would give Linda a tip-off.

I put the teapot on the step and saw the hole in the fence that separated the neighbour's yard at the back and ran for that hole. Unfortunately the dog saw me and grabbed me from behind. I fell and bumped my left knee, but I managed to pull myself from its grip and heard the sound of material tearing. I ran as fast as I could, and when I reached the corner, I noticed that half of my panty was hanging and my behind had burning scratches by the dog, displayed like a tattoo. My knee had a burning graze – the result of the violent fall. My mother choked with laughter when I told her what happened and took care of the bleeding wound. Nevertheless, whenever I saw Linda, I would change direction to avoid her and because I was shy for leaving her out in the 'cold'. Later on, Linda and I were on good terms again and I helped her many times to clean up.

During the rainy season all of us kids had a ball of a time after a heavy rainstorm. The rainwater would run down our street like a mini river. We had no tar roads then. The kids from the neighbourhood all gathered there and we played in that street river of ours. Cars could not use the road because it was too flooded and the current too strong. Later when the government needed to improve on the infrastructure we all knew that we would not have that river anymore. It was evident that the water would be rerouted through the storm pipe drain system. While they were busy working on the road, all of us would run behind the water truck for the sprinkles to shower our legs with the cool flow of water. However, one had to be careful not to slip in the mud, as it could cause devastating effects. We did not even consider in what danger we were placing ourselves; it was only about the fun but it was dangerous fun. One afternoon my mom saw us running behind the water truck and my brother and I received a good spanking. For me and my brother it was the end of our unusual shower sessions. The mischief was reported to the other parents and our comrades too were prospects of a spanking.

August month was known as the month of wind. My older brother and I would play with our kites with the other children from the neighbourhood. My other two siblings were not allowed to play on the field and could only watch us from the gate. I was always in a fight with the boys for damaging my kite with theirs. Nevertheless, life was not only about playing. When I was twelve years old, I helped Aunty Rose who was running a soup kitchen for the Anglican Church. I was responsible for slicing the bread because in those days sliced bread was not in fashion, and I can assure you there were many loaves to slice. Another youngster my age, also helping out, would butter the bread slice by slice in a sequence that really worked on my nerves, but Aunt Rose told me to be patient. Anyway, Aunty Rose would pour the soup into the plastic cups and the kids would then queue to collect their soup and come to the second line to collect their bread. What was so nice about the whole task was to watch with an undivided gaze how those underprivileged kids ate their bread and soup with much appreciation. I remembered how Uncle John, Aunty Rose's husband, would say to me as he watched me. 'Cut those slices, girl, for that is how you cast your bread upon the water, because after many days it shall return to you.' Sometimes the kids would have a treat when there was peanut butter available and they had a saying 'Today we are having bread in style.' Style it was because that was how they ate it – in style.

Those were beautiful days in my life because it was always worth my time and my effort. That was how communities operated in those days, always working together to help the underprivileged children of the area. So life was not only beautiful, life was sacred and full of love for the next person.

CHAPTER 1

Years later

It is so amazing for me to see the cycle and change of phases of my life. So how should we start? Once upon a time I was a cell that became a fetus and that fetus became a baby and I was born. It is a strong belief within me that something special was taking place elsewhere in the world at the time I entered into this world. Maybe an ice cap melted, a dewdrop slipped from a leaf, or a rainbow appeared in the sky. I am not exactly sure what happened but I do know it was an extraordinary beginning of life. So after the baby phase we go through the different seasons of our lives, as it is foreordained from the beginning of time. Time plays a big role in our lives — it is all about time.

Nevertheless, I recall the night before the first day I had to start school. My new uniform was neatly ironed, hanging on a hanger that was hooked into the handle of the wardrobe. I couldn't help but feel proud. My schoolbag was packed and many thoughts were racing through my mind. It was between excitement and a pinch of fear, nervously wondering about the many strangers I was going to meet. Would they be friendly, would they accept me, and what would the teacher be like? My brother who was already doing his third year told me not to worry because it was as easy as eating ice cream. Nonetheless, by the end of that first week I had many classmates. Primary school was fun.

Five years later when the cycle took another phase, I experienced the same feeling as the day I started school. I was older and it was my first year of senior secondary school. Again I admired my new uniform hanging from the wardrobe handle, only this time the thoughts racing through my mind were more severe. I was thinking about how time was moving on. It would be new faces and different teachers for each subject that would be taught. I was thinking that it would be a new phase of my life. Well, it was way different from primary school, but primary school was actually preparing one for high school. My brother again came to my rescue and dished out a prep-speech, which I appreciated. The one thing he said that was vital was to never procrastinate because the danger in falling behind would cause major problems for study purposes. He also spelled out that it was important to give the class projects on time because examination marks would be dependent on the project marks. It was a lot of information, but I always trusted my brother and took his word seriously. Needless to say, by the end of the first week I had many classmates and by the third month I joined the class study group. The cycle of my life had progressed onto another level. My brother was spot on when he warned me that the load of work was not to be underestimated. I tried hard to keep up and had to learn to write faster when the teachers explained their theories. Afternoon playing was limited because I had too much homework. With the result, my younger sister had to take over most of my chores.

Then came the matric year and again it was between excitement and that small dash of fear. I was excited to know that my school years were coming to an end and that I would enter into a new future to become a young adult. However, the important event to end the ten years of schooling would be the matric ball. But the biggest challenge was to pass matric; otherwise you had to rewrite and lose a year on your life. My brother passed his matric with flying colours and was already working and I had great admiration for him. But these are the cycles of life and it is amazing to look back and take stock. My brother prepared me for primary and high school; I prepared my younger sister and later she prepared our baby brother. We were a unit working together as a team. It was almost like the saying 'What goes around comes around'; the only difference was that what came around was good.

Anyway, in 1990 I completed my matric and passed with excellent results. Unfortunately for me, I did not apply for a bursary therefore I could not go to the university to study. I needed to get a job and work to save up money for my studies. As previously disadvantaged South Africans know, in those days the generation who were stepping into the world as young adults knew after school it was time to join the working class. I helped my mother at home with washing, cooking, and cleaning for a few months but it was time to work on my own future. The field that interested me was social work. It was a difficult regime for a non-white person, and the variety of options were limited. One could only apply for nursing, teaching, and the police force, etc. Those options did not interest me at all. It was not long when I heard from a friend that the Corporate Z had vacancies available. I saw an opportunity and I applied for a job. With the help of my matric certificate I was fortunate enough to be successful in my application. It was amazing to find myself working in a post office because it took me back to my childhood. I remembered how my brother-accompanied my mother to Kliptown post office. He would come back and tell how interesting it was to see when they stamped the documents with a bang. He said it gave him a thrill when the clerk hammered each document with fierce speed. He also collected the stamps from the old letters when my mother discarded the envelopes. My brother told me that the first postal stamp series of South Africa was issued on 31 May 1961 and he enjoyed himself explaining all the details that he knew by heart. In primary school we once had a lesson about the history of the Corporate Z and I enjoyed the topic with epic interest. It never crossed my mind that I would be the one working in the post office. It just shows that we are unable to stop fate.

I started as a sorter at Jeppe Street post office and was later transferred to Harrison Street depot. Six years later I was trained as a teller and worked at Booysens branch. After four years I was promoted as chief teller to Cresta post office; it was not long before I was promoted to branch manager and worked in that position for six years. My last office was in Weltevreden Park post office branch. So my whole life was about my work and I think it is safe for me to say that the post office became my life, my bread and butter. And I was quite aware of the fact that we only had a certain frame of time in that life to build a future. With much exuberance I worked very hard, building the progressive development of mine.

I can clearly remember the first time I received my first salary. There is no way that I will reveal the amount but at that time to me it was a small fortune. The important factor was the mere fact that I worked for it and I earned it with my sweat, my time, and maybe my skill, if one dares to call sorting letters a skill. The fact is that it was a job that added a contributing factor into the company's profitability and most importantly it was my job. Any job no matter how insignificant it might look in the eyes of others is important. In my personal opinion the person who earns money in an honest way is doing an important job.

Therefore, it might sound insignificant for others to describe my feelings about that day but it was on that day I became an adult with responsibilities. Yes, I was stepping into a new phase of my time into a life-changing experience prepared just for me – a transformation. With pride I walked through the doors of the bank to change my cheque. I remember having spunk in every step I took. Yes, I was proud of my achievement and myself. Nevertheless, I opened a bank account in my name so that in the next round, my salary would be directly paid into my account. When all my documents were completed and approved I could withdraw money. I withdrew my boarding and a small sum for my bus ticket. My mind went back to the day when I had told my siblings that the day I went to work I would buy only chocolates with my whole salary. It was not that way now but it was a sense of joy to know that I could now take care of my own finances. Of course, I had a bank account in my own name. Knowing this filled me with such an unexplainable sense of happiness and satisfaction. This was the result of a fresh achievement. I was facing the future now in the shoes of an adult and for the first time I saw life had meaning and purpose. One can only perceive the moment with gratefulness because that day was documented not only in my conscious mind but also as an instant of my history.

My mother was proudly smiling when I handed her the envelope with my gratification and spoke to me about the importance of budgeting. My father gave me a long speech about saving a few rand every month so that I could later buy a car. I will never forget that moment of so much importance and self-worth. In addition, the main thing for me to see was how proud my parents were of me. My mom was the caring housewife keeping the family together and making sure we were all fine. With four children not very far apart in age, there certainly was no gap for her to have a job – she already had one. If I jot it down now, then I must say she worked in many departments on a freelance basis. She was a chef, a home executive, and a day-care teacher. Her contribution to her family was unselfish, and she rendered her service with unconditional love. My younger sister and I had chores and would take turns to wash the dishes at night. My father worked hard in the building industry and never wanted his family to be deprived of anything. From a tender age we were taught values and we were very family-orientated. As a family we were always supporting one another and that was why my parents could sit me down and advise me. Anyway, the following week I opened my first clothing account to at least build references to have credibility for later purchases. The excitement was overwhelming and I was excited to sign for my first purchase. These are the important memories in my life that I will never forget.

In 1995, I bought a house through the post office where I am currently residing. I was twenty-three years of age at the time. My parents were proud to see that I invested my money in a property. Then came the season of love; cupid shot his arrow straight into my heart. I met a man and like all young adults my age, we fell in love. We dated for an year and I became pregnant with my first child, a baby girl whom I named Agatha. My parents were not very happy about the news of pregnancy because I was depriving them of a *white wedding*, but they said nothing. I could only imagine that they had high hopes for me and that I had messed up their plans. Nevertheless, in this life it is of great importance that one could never live up to the expectations of others because we do not know what the future holds.

However, as the months proceeded my mother helped me prepare for the new bundle of joy that was about to enter our lives. I had a medical aid that was covering the medical expenses. With months passing by, I became more and more excited about my impending motherhood. It would be a new season of my life but my family was my support system.

Then came the expected day after the patient wait. Agatha was born on 12 May 1997 and she became the highlight of my life. My family was happy for me and because I was not married she was registered under my family name. Later my relationship with Agatha's father became sour and he left without an explanation. This was a sad time in my life. It was most likely for me to feel lost and lonely but I knew one thing; that I was always strong and had to be stronger now for the sake of my child. My baby's father left me at a time when I needed him the most to be a father for our baby and a helpmate to me. All the same, that is life and it does not always run smooth. I decided to live through the pain and tears to tackle all life's problems on my own.

I am happy to say that by the grace of the Almighty I survived. And fortified by the principles of my life, I was an excellent single mother, patient and hard-working. I had a good job and thrived on it. I had a car and a house. I paid my bills on time and whenever I looked into my daughter's eyes I had reason to smile. Yes, above all things I was most richly blessed. My daughter's father lived his own life and did not really have enough time for her. But, I was there – not only to rear and look out for her, but also to love her. She became my first priority and I liked it that way. It was a hard road to travel alone but my siblings were my great support system. After my maternity leave my mother offered to look after my daughter and I went back to work.

Being at work and knowing my baby was at home was again another hurdle for me to overcome. I felt guilty but realized that there were bills that had to be paid. Notwithstanding, my joy would return when it was time to knock off, knowing that I was going home to my beautiful baby girl. It was a feeling of pride, love, and the responsibility of being someone's mama. I think all mothers can relate to me. Once you have given birth to your first child your life changes in many unexpected ways. It is as if you have suddenly grown so fast. Your way of thinking is different and you are always on the edge, worried and concerned whether you were doing things right. Everything you measure with caution. Bottles and clothes are taken care of with concentration not to use the wrong detergents. My favourite was folding the soft blankets. Your whole world changes because it is all about the little one now. The Mama trigger is in place and you want to do everything right. You look at those two eyes, the fingers, toes, and nose, and you ask yourself silently, 'Is this really true?'. Life has many cycles and I was now in the cycle of motherhood. My life was about my job and my baby now and it felt good. Unfortunately, our lives were disorientated by unforeseen catastrophes.

With much dedication and pride I saw my daughter grow. The growing phases we went through together was as if we were a team that wanted to succeed. I felt whole and proud that God had entrusted that baby into my care. I experienced the love of a mother and it helped me to appreciate my mother more. It stood as proof that I learned so much from my mother and my mother was proud to be of such great help. As for me, it was a privilege to learn the skills of motherhood from my mother – I got first-hand practices.

Eight years later my daughter's father came back, and I being such a forgiving person gave him another chance. In my mind I created this *dream* that it would work out this time. I was happy simply because now my child would have her daddy and it would save me from all the questions I have to answer. I didn't know what it was like to grow up without a father, but I had friends who went through that circumstances and I had seen their emotional turmoil. I saw how my daughter connected with her daddy and it all looked so right. It all went good and well for the first few months. He played his role as a father and a lover but then I noticed the restlessness in him. He became impatient with Agatha and got easily irritated. He started complaining about my cooking and minor things about the household. Many times I was about to question him about the things that made him unhappy but I was too tired to fuss about it. Then came the unexpected news. I was pregnant with my second child; again I was disappointed because the man left me again.

On 28 February 2005, God blessed me with another baby girl, Amy. Agatha accepted that her father was not around anymore. However, she was more focused on her little sister and promised me that she would help me raise this new bundle of joy. I did not bother to ask my ex to come see the new baby, because this baby was mine. This time I was well prepared and again my mother came to my rescue. My mother is a real hero in my life and I sometimes fail to let her know her worth. I see how she rears my children with love and patience. She is always so passionate about their well-being. To my mother all her grandchildren are her life and she has no favourites; she loves them all in the same way. Truly saying, my mother's children are blessed to have her as a mother and all our babies are blessed too because they have a grandma in a million.

My life did not go according to how I planned it, but through it all, I had learnt to trust God and he was my saving grace. Again, I went through the same sequence with my newborn without the man who fathered her but it was fine. This time I was so hurt at being left alone in the lurch that I found myself crying at night. I questioned myself time and again and felt guilty for making the wrong choice for the second time. What was more painful was when Agatha phoned her dad and he would promise to visit or take her out but would not turn up, seeing how my child would wait the whole day all dressed up and ready but waiting in vain. I saw how she walked up and down to the gate to see if her daddy was perhaps waiting outside. She would come back into the house to watch TV but would look at her watch every five minutes. The waiting was more about stress for her. It was not at all pleasant for me to see. Later she got so used to the silly game that when he called and made all his promises to her she would just talk and listen to him but would not wait. I heard her say one day that she did not think her daddy loved her. All this made me feel so guilty and sad because I blamed myself for the situation that my child was in. I came to the realization that my guilt would destroy me and make me depressed. It was time to turn things around because my babies needed a sane, strong mother. With the help of prayer I did exactly that and I become stronger as the days went by.

Through this book my friends and siblings will know who I really am. I never had a sad look on my face, never complained, and never talked about how personal situations affected me. We think the world is too busy and people don't care, but there are people who can surprise us sometimes, like in my case. One woman read my silence, took note of my body language, looked deep into my eyes, and saw my silent emotional pain.

My deep emotional pain clouded my mind and made my eyesight dim. I struggled with my own questions and search for answers. Nevertheless, this super lady could see what I tried hard not to make visible. She spoke to me with an indescribable connection and being questioned by her made me pour out what was hidden deep inside. For the first time I could offload without worry and really I did. I was given an opportunity to speak and complain because someone was prepared to listen and cry with me. That is why I decided to open up by doing this project. I have bottled up all my emotions; everything was imploded and by putting my story on paper it gives me a chance to explode and break this silence. For way too long I was held up in my perfect little prison. The prison of guilt and blame that makes me see my dreams only in a distant horizon. I regard this project a platform to have my say and I am going to do so loud and clear. I do not want to be seen; I want to be heard.

On my own I always had to evaluate what needed to be done and would just do it on my own. I always felt that I should never burden others with my problems. I always hid my vulnerability to focus on dealing with things myself but that was not always good. No man is an island; we need an outlet pipe to talk and offload at one stage or the other, but that was not what I did. I tried my best to keep it sane and in balance. Maybe I tried too hard to be the architect of my life. One cannot build a house on one's own. So I was taking things too hard on my own.

What groomed me in my young life was that I always had a positive and hopeful outlook. It was always in my interest to loosen up my ideas and ideals of what would work best for me. Herewith, I was the kind of person who was always so careful in providing for my future; no task was ever unworthy for me to do.

But the one thing I did not do was to leave a little space for disappointment and found that I was unprepared for the unexpected. I never thought I would ever find myself on the *battleground*, because I lived a simple, quiet life. I went to work, church, school meetings, and visited friends and family.

Occasionally I would take the kids to a movie or on an excursion. Life was not all gloomy but I had accomplished much because I was focused. And I had this remarkable energy that kept me motivated to live and learn. Together with this, I was always blessed with friends around me. My friends knew how to party and some weekends we would party until the break of day. Yes, I can openly say I enjoyed my life. At times I look at my kids and see their innocence; then I cannot help but wonder whether they too would be rebellious like I was. We all have that streak when we go through our growing-up stages. I remember my rebellion of bunking school or certain classes, especially if I didn't have my homework. I must admit that I gave my teachers grief because I had to go with the flow. You need to be in the game otherwise your peers will find you to be boring, so you take on the trend so as not to be seen as a bore.

When I was in standard eight, on Friday nights my friends and I would go to Club Status (the local nightclub at the time). We were drinking, smoking, hooking up with guys, and dancing the night away. The story I gave at home was that we practiced for the school concert, which never existed. The challenge was how to get back into the house in the early hours of the mornings without my parents having to see that I was intoxicated. During school holidays we would group up and go camping. Other holidays I would accompany my mother to the province where she was born, to visit family. During those visits I would go out with my cousins on picnics and nightclubs. Sadly, we youngsters made the adults worry if we were not home by twelve at night. What they did not know was that for us youngsters, the fun only started at twelve; that was the time our parties started bumping and by then we would all be intoxicated. By the time we arrived home it would be three or six in the morning. With the result, we would be tired, drunk, and very boisterous, using a collection of many unrefined words as a matter of self-defence to sidestep any queries. One Sunday morning my uncle did not take any nonsense from any of us and we were quickly sorted out with his leather waist belt. The next weekend we all remained indoors and watched movies. Thinking of it now, occasional hidings helped tone down rebellion.

My mother told me that one day I too would sit up waiting for my children the way she did. I can only imagine that she did the same to her mother and knew what her mother went through at that time. She said that my rebellion now was what I sowed, but one day I would reap the very same. However, it was the sequence of all young people to enjoy themselves. I was young and irresponsible.

Those were the little stunts I managed to pull off. Fortunately for me the naughtiness only lasted for a while because I really wanted to excel in school and finish my matric. I was a top student and an excellent athlete and my parents expected me to keep up with that standard. I wanted to please them and really I tried.

But Jesus said, Suffer little children, and forbid
them not, to come unto me: for of such is the
kingdom of heaven.

Matthew 19:14

CHAPTER 2

Fifteenth December 2009 – a date I will never forget as long as I live. We normally do the banking between 3 and 4 p.m. in the afternoon. After I do the banking, I call the assistant (checking officer) in to double-check, witness, and seal the stop-loss bags for the money collectors to collect. One bag is for the money and the other bag is for cheques only. The collectors would take the bags from us to the bank. Everything was in order and we placed the bags in the lockable space on the shelves in the safe. Every office has what we call a walk-in strong room and in that strong room was my safe and safes for the tellers. Now myself, the assistant, and all other tellers have access to the strong room. The reason is that the tellers have to collect money and credit cards to hand over to the clients when they collected. That was how it worked and we all followed the sequence.

Later that day the security officers arrived to collect the bags to take to the bank like every other day. I went to the strong room to take the bags to hand over to the collectors. To my surprise the one bag that contained the money was open. Now this was very unusual because the assistant had sealed both bags in my presence earlier. I called her and she too was surprised. She carefully inspected the bag and we both discovered that the bag was different. How we knew that was because there was a certain way to seal the bags and the one who had swapped it did not know how to seal the bag. The blood was rushing to my head, the anxiety building up like a flood. I felt paralyzed and was speechless. 'What now?' I thought.

With trembling hands we opened the bag and looked inside and were now more amazed. Inside we discovered paper neatly cut into the size of money notes, heaped up with elastic bands to hold it together. It was exactly the way we did the banking. The paper that was used was that of the 'yellow pages – the phone directory'. Wow! How nicely planned. The assistant and I realised that the money bag had been swapped. It was highly impossible that this exercise could have been done on site. We looked at each other and knew who the thief was. A young girl had been employed a few months ago and from the time she had been part of the staff we had had many complaints. Staff complained that they were missing money from their purses and stock from the strong room. Because no one could prove it, we all just made sure that we kept our money and personal belongings in our lockers or pockets. It was not our place to take her out.

I had no other option but to tell the collectors to leave because there was no money to hand over. By now, the chaos in the office was hectic. I then decided not to give the cheques yet because the money was missing. However, I could not hold the collectors from their other duties. I placed the bag with the cheques back in the safe and went to my desk to think.

For the first time in my history of working for the Corporate Z, money got stolen out of the safe by one of my employees. The reason why I say one of my employees is because there was no burglary. So it was my duty to report the matter to the South African Police Force and to the investigation department of the company. I made all the other necessary reports and called the police.

I became aware that everything for me at work could just spiral out of control. I would be blamed because I was in charge. It would be a hard time for me because I knew what was coming next – a hearing, which was fair and maybe a court order. Where would all this end and would it end and when would it end?

I sat in my office, shocked, benumbed in silent confusion. I felt desolate and felt like a stranger in a foreign country where no one knows you. For at that moment no one came near me to even support me. I suppose the staff felt I should be left alone. Or was everyone as confused as I was at the time. There was a void in me. Never in my life had I felt so alone and weak. I suddenly feared the future, my future. What would happen to my job, my babies, my house, and me? What an explosion of change and it was most calamitous because it was an embarrassing reflection pointing at me. I was really strained and confused. I tried hard to think how this incident could have happened. I quietly prayed to God with lost hope. The walk-in safe had a lockable steel door and the inside of the safe was partitioned by mesh wire into two separate areas.

One area had a separate lockable section with a mesh safe door where cash was kept. But how and when did all this take place was my question to myself.

That night I did not go straight home like always. I went to a friend who was also working for the Corporate Z, but at another branch. I needed to talk things over. Through my tears I told her about my ordeal. She tried hard to support me and talked to me at length. I could not stop myself from crying. In life we as humans all cry for different reasons but the colour of tears are the same.

When I left from my friend I went to my sister that night and we prayed together. My sister too had worked for some time at Kliptown office and she knew the sequence of daily duties. Again I cried and cried because my life was in dire need of providence. In my throat there was a painful lump. It was as if all my emotions were blocked in the lump in my throat. I asked God for direction and to help me to deal with the confrontation that was awaiting me. I sat on the bed and gave this whole situation much thought. I was trying to figure out how the swap of the bag had happened but I struggled to think clearly. Sleep would not come; my sister gave me pills because my head was throbbing and it was as if it wanted to burst. I could not control how I felt, and I walked up and down in the passage like an insane person. It is hard to explain the feeling and I can just imagine what other people had to endure when this kind of incident happened to them. I would not even want to wish such a situation on an enemy if I have one.

Did one ever learn to know one's friend or foe? Was this the masterpiece of my disaster? No one knows when trouble strikes. We cannot always say one will be prepared for the unexpected. Here I was now with what I had never expected and somehow I wished I were dead.

For me this was bad, worse than the time my children's father abandoned me. My whole world started to change in a way I never expected. I asked myself so many questions to understand where in my life did I go wrong. Now I blamed myself for not being alert enough and the catastrophe haunted me. Every night at home I was miserable and worried; it affected my health and I experienced a lot of pains in my legs. My strength was suffering a lot of abuse and I was mentally exhausted. When things are all fine in our lives we never really predict critical transition that can occur overnight.

Despite this sudden shift and anything to the contrary I learned to occupy myself with household chores and at night I helped my children with homework and school projects. Yes, my children kept me sane and I thanked God for having them because without them my life would have been empty, especially now. Right now they were the ones keeping my head above the water. I had to stand strong.

Anyway, many meetings were held and I was always left in the dark, not knowing what to expect. Every day I went about my job responsibilities like every normal day, trying hard not to worry about the outcome. But something always remained obscure, and deep down, I just could not help but be afraid. I was not only afraid but I was also starting to hate. I suppose it was human nature and not a sign of weakness. So here I was in a place where I never imagined I would be and I beg you to journey with me through this unpleasant ordeal and meet me, feel me, and remember me.

For thou art my hope, O Lord God: thou art my trust from my youth.

Psalm 71:5

CHAPTER 3

Meet me – the woman with the Broken Face.

They did not slap me in my face. They did not even pull the skin off my face; no, they broke my face. My name is Sandra and I am the woman with the Broken Face, the crushed heart, and the blood tears. I am an object of an unfair dismissal, charged but proven wrong. Cast down but not forsaken by my God, therefore I will be like David and prepare my pebbles to go to battle with the great Goliath. I am ready for this battle but I plan to win the war because I know that I am innocent. The day I was dismissed, I did not die and while there is life in this body of mine, I will fight until the end of this unpleasant journey.

I am not the perpetrator here. I am an innocent victim; therefore, I cannot step back and accept this unjust treatment.

I think it is safe for me to say, 'I was in the wrong place at the wrong time and on the wrong day.' My fight back will set an example that in this life you are only guilty until proven so. One cannot walk away without closure because the truth is there to set you free. I was robbed of my liberation and was left to feel worthless and condemned. My name was tarnished and I was stripped of my dignity, while the guilty person just reported sick and resigned one month before the hearing. I reported to my superiors that she was a suspect but she was never investigated. Anyway, it came as no surprise because I was already the chosen victim.

I was well groomed and came from a very decent background. We were not rich but also not poor. My dad was a hard-working man and my mom became a housewife after my brother's birth. We grew up in a home where we were loved and taken care of. So why should I allow certain people to condemn me, treat me unjustly, and think that they can get away with it? Sorry, that is not going to happen.

Knowing that my superiors held many meetings privately discussing my future within the Corporate Z made me worried. The days went by in much anticipation. I was waiting for a hearing date. It was imperative for me to know where I stood and just get all this behind me. I was still under the impression that they would consider my years with the post office and the fact that I had never had any pending cases. Little did I know what was waiting for me. People never care about you when they are done with you and that's the hard reality. Nevertheless, hard realities are what you find out when you are in a crisis – it is the cycle of life. Depending on one's crisis and the emanation it gives is always the one thing that drives you to see it through, no matter the mental abuse you suffer. It's a matter of doing what you have to do and believe in one's heart that there is always hope. In my opinion now, if I allow anyone to bully me then I make him or her the winner and I will be the loser standing alone – the lame one. But like I said, I am here to win because I want no nonsense with my name.

Then came the day of the hearing.

The Disciplinary Enquiry

After eight months of emotional torture the big day arrived. The date, 29 November 2010, will always be fresh in my mind. Imagine how they waited to dismiss me just before the Christmas season. It was like a catastrophic explosion that took place. I was cross-questioned, disrespected, and ostracized; then I had to endure nasty looks of disbelief. It was as if I was on trial for murder. I listened and observed how I was humiliated for something I had not done. In my mind many questions came to the fore. What happened to the solid rock of humanity where another human is his brother's keeper? What happened to the pathway of justice and fairness? What happened to the soul force of dignity and discipline? Have the hearts of all human beings suddenly waxed cold? Confusion, despair, and disappointment were immediately activated in my mind.

The way they questioned me asking the same thing over and over in a different way as if I was an idiot, made me feel degraded. Was it their way of interrogation? Well, if so, then I thought it was worse than the National Intelligence. I was literally stalked, mentally abused, and poked with a hot poker, like the ones we used in those Welcome Dover coal stoves in earlier days. I was not even asked to say something in defence for myself; no, my voice did not count but I knew my statement was in writing. 'They look at me as the offender and think they own my soul, how sad,' I thought to myself. 'My world will not end here and they will not govern my life.'

Was this the new democracy I was living in where you could see how your life was stolen away from you by an unjust treatment? I had a family that had freedom fighters who fought long for justice and here I sat and experienced injustice myself and on my own.

It was clear to me that my life was being invaded by stone-cold human beings whose minds were already made up. This, to me, was a massive storm and after this storm there would be no rainbow for me. It was right then that I knew that the situation was going to be bad for me. I made my mind up right there. It was time to rise up and not accept defeat. I will rearrange this situation and use my rights as a citizen of this beautiful country. I had been too nice for too long now; I remove the 'n' from the nice and I am like ice. Like the freedom fighters who fought for the freedom of the oppressed so will I fight for my name. I never expected to see a time in my life where I had to fight to prove my innocence. There was enough spirit within me; therefore, I would cling to my pride and fight back like a wounded animal. Yes, I was wounded – in my soul. I would get this done through the power of my emotional commitment. With faith I would aggressively fight to accomplish the goals inspired by the faces I now look at – a nasty sight and vermin enough to make me press on towards my mark. These were the people who had placed their trust in me for many years. As for now they saw me the way they wanted to see and heard me the way they wanted to hear. Furthermore, they were the people whom I served with dignity and trustworthy business ethics. Sadly, now they treated me like a criminal. For this reason, I was now a rebel with a cause and my truth was my truth. For one, I was not a thief and I shall give no one the authority to see me as one. For now it was as the saying went, 'You strike a woman – you strike a rock'. I was that rock now. The power of willingness was present now and it would be wrong for me to just simply resist this willingness to defend myself. The truth was, to walk away and call it quits would make me feel defeated. Not only was it my duty but it was also my constitutional right to help correct the error. It might offend many but I was only reacting to the willingness within. Remember, I was fighting for my bread and butter because if I didn't I would never be employed again in the Republic of South Africa. What would happen to me then? Therefore, the willingness had made a satisfying choice and I was going to please myself knowing that I was standing up for what was right. Nothing should deny me from doing so because it was my democratic right. Not only as a citizen but also as a human being.

After long deliberation, then came the shocking news, the hard reality. I was dismissed on the grounds of *gross negligence* and it was exactly what I thought they would use against me. According to them, I was in charge of the branch and the company took a loss. The second charge was because I did not hand over the cheques to the security officers. My tears wanted to do a freestyle but I held them back. I had had enough humiliation for one day and I would not want these people to have the privilege of seeing my tears.

After eight months of misery and uncertainty I now heard this. The word 'dismissal' sent down shock waves through my whole body. My blood was streaming faster through my veins. My emotions were acting up and it felt as if I'd lost the ownership of myself. Was this a deliberate act of omission? Because they did not even try to defend me as an employee of their company. Or did they defend me and this was only how I felt. Some of their comments evoked protest in my mind but I said nothing. I was merely a humble listener, listening to how I was a seasoned branch manager but acted negligently.

I knew myself as a very reasonable and honest person. I was loyal and ethical to every branch where I worked, and I sat there and had to hear that I was dismissed because I was negligent. I saw nothing now; I saw only the letters in bold – *Termination of Service.*

Who did those people think they were? Didn't they fear God? Did they really think I would just accept defeat and walk away without a fight? No one could play me like this with my children's bread and think they could get away with it. Looking at their faces made me hate them. It was a hatred that could make no way for sympathy. Twenty years of my life was being compromised with. Getting up and looking at them was so painful, they showed no remorse; they were just simply a cold, hostile audience. I could not help but think that this was a pain pattern that was passed on to many before me. But this was now in my time and only time knows now. I stared and imagined that according to them I had disgraced the company. But to me, they were a disgrace to the human race.

I left the meeting with a broken heart but a sound mind. That day when I walked out of the doors of my branch, I was in a daze. I walked out and every step I took was heavy. I looked back and it was as if a sharp pain slowly penetrated my heart.

The tears I held back during the hearing was now running down my cheeks as I walked away. I tasted my tears – it tasted bitter. I felt powerless and defeated, a feeling I would not even wish on my enemy. Travelling home, I gathered all my thoughts to do some mitigation. By the time I reached the gate of my house my mind was made up.

I knew what I was going to do. A week after my dismissal I reported my case to the CCMA (Commission for Conciliation, Mediation and Arbitration). The CCMA took my case on the grounds that my representative contested the substantive fairness of the dismissal. I then had to wait for a date for the next hearing. Weeks and months passed and I waited in great anticipation. I tried hard to manage the wait but I feared the future. Day after day I tried to look for the inner silence to find peace but my mind found no rest.

When the time arrived for the case hearing, my representing party notified me that they preferred reinstatement as a remedy. I was happy with the decision and gave the go-ahead. But still I had to wait. In the meantime my life savings I had was slowly drying up. All these years working, I had saved up money the way my father had advised me to do when I received my first salary. Nevertheless, months were passing by; I paid the bond of my house with my savings and made arrangements with the bank. I was quite aware that later on I would fall into trouble with payments but I would cross that bridge when I got there. I could not settle my other small accounts and I was blacklisted. The commission of the beauty products I sold was not enough to sustain us but it helped. It was not easy because I had always provided for my family and I was not used to asking people for help. This whole saga I saw was teaching me new life strategies. I learnt to appreciate every piece of bread and every rand I turned around and respected the fact of having it. I took the time to sometimes wonder if I was maybe selfish and wasteful now God was teaching me a lesson. Was it my time to go through the fiery furnace of fire in order to reach my perfection to be more humane? However, I focused my thoughts on what was the most important payment and that was the roof over my head so that I didn't have to be homeless. With all that stress I had to cope with while I was waiting in anticipation for my name to be cleared, my body was feeling the liquidation of change.

O my God, I trust in thee: let me not be
ashamed, let not mine enemies triumph over me.

Psalm 25:2

CHAPTER 4

One afternoon I got a call from an unknown number. I did not know the caller, but he told me he was prepared to testify on my behalf because he knew the thief. He also said that he was an accomplice in the theft and he wanted to teach the thief a lesson because he didn't get his cut of the money. He was prepared to bring out every detail of how the theft took place. I listened with caution but became suspicious when he wanted to meet with me alone and told me that I should not discuss this call with anybody. I then told him to give me time to think about it and when I asked for his number he told me that I shouldn't worry because he would phone me. After we ended the call, I immediately made an appointment with my extended family because now I was worried and I feared for my life. How stupid did this guy think I was? Yes, I was stupid when the money disappeared at my branch, but this was a no-no. Really! I was the woman with the Broken Face but I was no fool. As for his cut of the money . . . duh! It was because of that stolen money that I was out of my job. Did they think of my future and now he wanted me to help so that he could get his revenge?

Was this girl who swapped the bag angry because of the way I approached her that day of the incident? Now recalling the details of that day I remembered going to the suspect. This was how I did it because I too was scared.

'Please! Just give me the money, and I will not report it. We will just forget about it and regard it as a mistake.' The suspect looked at me and laughed in my face. I turned to walk away and my left arm accidently brushed her chin because she was sitting down. I looked back at her but did not say sorry. So maybe she held that against me and wanted me to pay for the humiliation by sending guys after me to actually hurt me. I wished that one day I could meet the thief just to confront her with one question and that is – Why?

I now strongly felt that at the time I reported her to my superiors as a suspect, they should have investigated her with immediate effect. But no, they just wanted to see me as the thief or was it a good opportunity for them to get rid of me because of my age and my years in the company? Sorry! But I am only speculating and stand corrected. I mean it is my right, isn't it? Because I am the woman who has sleepless nights and muscle pains because I am the accused here. Nevertheless, why does such things have to happen with decent citizens? People who uphold the law and who know how to treat others with politeness. Was it not unfair or was I wrong? Was I looking for sympathy? Yes, I did; I deserved a bit of sympathy because I felt cheated by some people, the system, and life. I felt abused, degraded, betrayed, and above all, humiliated. I was not sure if it was all part of life or was it just meant only for me. But I pledged to myself to decline the venom of the criminal mind (the caller) to be injected into my soul. Let them find better prospects from another victim but it would not be me. Could I have so much trouble in my life and still set myself out as a meal ticket – no way.

That Friday night I was in Bassonia and told my extended family exactly word for word about the conversation of the unknown caller. They advised me not to even consider it because my case was at the CCMA and that I should tell them to rather call the police. It was not wise to make any deals with a criminal, because a criminal has no conscience. Criminals are the players on the Devil's ground and I was just a woman who wanted to prove my innocence. Nevertheless, I never heard from the mysterious caller again. It showed that there was an agenda because his syndicate thought that the bait would entice me because I was desperate. This was exactly my point – the morals of people had taken a turn for the worse. Would God help me to stay within my limits as a human being even though I was paining and bleeding with the turmoil of my situation? Would I remember that vengeance was never mine? Would I learn to forgive and forget and remember that I had a soul that was precious in the eyes of God! Was there no place to hide? And where could one run? Had the well-being of another's life become so worthless or do others think it had become their basic right to make life difficult for the next person? Wow, in which galaxy are we? And was the spirit of Cain back with us answering 'Am I my brother's keeper'? Anyway, that night I had terrible nightmares because my mind was now traumatised with the fear that was instilled in me with the phone call of the unknown caller.

Then again, life went on and I waited for the outcome of my case. I was on the waiting list and it had become second nature to me. Now I knew how Nelson Mandela had felt waiting for his long walk to freedom, yet I went through but a fraction of his suffering. So now you sense what I the woman with the Broken Face must have felt. I say this, because as you read you are in my shoes and with great respect I appreciate the fact that you journey with me. This is not the greatest problem in the world but it is my problem and you don't need to feel sorry for me because you know about worse things than what I am going through now. Think of me as nothing but I was just a woman driven to the point of desperation fighting to restore my dishonoured name and my self-worth, the value of who I was. I am nothing special; I am only another inhabitant of the earth but I too have the right to be here. I quote the *Desiderata* – a child of the universe. Yes, I am a member of civilization and a legal citizen of this country. If you think I am petty then I say, 'Yes, you are right, and yes, there are more major situations out there in the world. But bear with me as a mother and just another human being. This is my cross and I must carry it.' Like I said, I am nothing special but I am somebody's mother and that makes a difference. Therefore, I appreciate what you feel for me, and I might not know who you are but the fact that you continue to read this book is highly appreciated. I know that many will think that I am attacking the Corporate Z but that is not the case here. I am fighting for my honour and my job, and under the circumstances, I speak from my heart and I utter out my pain.

In my understanding what is sacred is never for sale and my truth is sacred. That is why people swear by the truth even in the court of law but I live by it. Therefore, I will never exchange my truth for something else because my truth is who

I am and which will set me free to put the record straight. I pray to God that my truth will be seen and accepted by my accusers and hope for their apology.

It seems to me that in this life the criminal stands a better chance of being believed. Has the legal system failed us all or has some demonic force disrupted the mindset of people? I wish I had all the answers to my own questions but I know life has its own cycle that we have no access to. It is tiring to feel this way with the fear and confusion but I will have to bear the weight until the hearing is conducted.

Who is as the wise man? and who knoweth the interpretation of a thing? a man's wisdom maketh his face to shine, and the boldness of his face shall be changed.

Ecclesiastes 8:1

CHAPTER 5

Months Later the hearing was conducted.

The Hearing

By now I had a case number and a CCMA (Commission for Conciliation, Meditation and Arbitration) case number as well. The hearing was conducted under the auspices of the CCMA in Johannesburg on Tuesday, 5 April 2011. The proceedings were conducted in terms of Section 191 of the Labour Relations Act 66/1995 (The Act) as amended.

Issue in dispute regarding the dismissal of Sandra that was occasioned on 29 November 2010. Dismissal was for a reason associated with the Employee's conduct: Whether the dismissal of Sandra was fair or not and the applicable remedy, if any.

Both parties were represented during the arbitration proceedings. (Please note that I hereby do not wish to use any names of representatives for the sake of privacy)

Here is a short background of the dispute:

Here is the case of the Employer in short.

a) The company suffered a loss of R42,000.
b) The loss was attributed to the Employee's negligence.
c) The Employee's negligence manifested itself in the Employee's failure to safeguard the Employer's assets.
d) The Employee's failure to make a bank deposit of cheques valued at R61,000 on the same day of collection being 15 December 2009.
e) The Employee's conduct constituted grave misconduct and the dismissal penalty was appropriate taken into account the consequences of the Employee's conduct.

Nevertheless, here is the scale I contested on the following basis:

a) The Employer had failed to prove that I the Employee was negligent let alone grossly negligent.
b) I the Employee had acted with diligence and had to this end complied with the prescribed operations and banking procedure.
c) I the Employee had made numerous attempts through the area manager to acquire a stand-alone safe but without success.
d) Pilfering was a common occurrence in the walk-in safe area which factor had prompted me, the Employee, to request for a stand-alone safe. A stand-alone safe

would in the Employee's view have been more suitable for the safekeeping of items of value such as cash, credit cards, and cheques.

e) My failure to bank the cheques within the described period was due to circumstances not of my own making.

f) My failure to do the banking in the prescribed manner could at most amount to non-compliances with policy and not an act of negligence as contemplated in the Employer's disciplinary code.

Furthermore, the lady who has done the investigation (she was in the service of the Employer) testified that she observed the burglar door leading to the walk-in safe was unlocked during her investigation. She also said that all employees had the freedom to walk in and out of the walk-in safe. According to the investigator this fact was communicated to senior management through her investigation report and she led evidence on this point in the pre-dismissal enquiry.

In addition, the investigator's version in this regard was not supported by the facts. In fact, the investigation report was not presented as evidence and the minutes of the enquiry made no reference to the burglar door left open and members of the staff having unlimited access to the walk-in safe.

Nevertheless, I profoundly rejected the version of the investigator because it was not consistent with the facts and was not convincing. Furthermore, her version lacked credibility. To make a long story short, in his submission the Employer's representative argued that my dismissal stemmed from my failure of safeguarding the assets of the company.

However, the Commissioner found that the Employer's representative was being unfair in even suggesting that failure to the safeguard was at issue in the enquiry and that the charge of gross negligence suggests that my conduct deviated from the norm which was not the case. The Commissioner also mentioned that there was no concrete evidence verbal or written to suggest that I had breached any set of operations. To sum up the foregoing, it was the finding of the Commissioner that the Employer exploited its position of power by terminating my services on the basis of mere suspicion.

It was taken from what the Employer's representative said: 'The Employer's case was based on suspicion that because the Employee, by leaving the burglar door unlocked, presented an opportunity for someone to sneak in and remove the cash.

'To me that already was an accusation without any proof or substance because the investigation did not confirm its suspicions. In conclusion the Employer had no reason to pursue the so-called negligence charge in the absence of supporting evidence. As for the question in respect of banking could have been adequately addressed with disciplinary action short of dismissal if there were no justifying circumstances in the name of failing to comply in terms of the disciplinary code.'

Section 192(2) of the Act makes express provision that the onus to establish the fairness of a dismissal rests with an employer. Where misconduct is at issue an employer must prove the existence of a reason to dismiss, such as gross misconduct and the fairness of the reason or the misconduct as a reason to dismiss.

However, in closing the Commissioner's findings were as follows.

'Accordingly I find that the Employer had without justification, irrationally and unreasonably infringed the Employee's right not to be unfairly dismissed.'

The Award from the CCMA:

'The dismissal was unfair. I therefore order the Corporate ∠ to reinstate Sandra on or before 3 May 2011.'

With this said, I was elated with the outcome of the case and really thought that my trouble was over, but I was wrong. I was found not guilty, but then the company (Employer) had enough nerve to depose the ruling of the CCMA and referred the case to the Labour Court for further review. The order from the CCMA was made for me to be reinstated, but sixteen months later I still found myself unemployed and struggling to make ends meet. My house was about to be auctioned. There were mouths to feed and bills to pay, but the company I gave my life and dedication to could not be bothered. Who was I after all? I was dismissed. And why should they care about me?

To exemplify, I was quite aware what they were doing. I had seen it so many times with other victims and I am sure that I will be criticised for saying this but I am saying it anyhow because I am an angry woman.

They want you to lose your house and car, and then you get blacklisted for non-payment and that will be the end of your credibility. Your name will then be listed with the credit bureau.

I have seen victims losing their families, their minds, and their dignity, and then they simply become hobos. Marriages end and children go astray because the lives of the innocent were stolen away in a twinkling of an eye. I know of people with similar cases and are still without employment. No one wants to employ them because of their records. It becomes hard for some of these victims to cope with the serious financial burden they face, and many will just put an end to their lives to escape the emotional pain. They don't know how to break the *silence of abuse* and how to defend themselves against the powerful, highly educated, and the rich. Therefore, they just give up on life. Some victims are offered ridiculous settlements and because of the desperation they are faced with, they take it and walk away. The sad part, however, is that they will never get employed anywhere in the Republic of South Africa again.

Now how fair is that and how can it end? So if no one is prepared to break this silence then we will all just be silenced and perish together. Here is where I come in, because I will be a fugitive to no one. I put myself out as the sacrifice because if I don't fight back I will be doing myself a great injustice. Not that I can save the world and not that I am able to rewrite the work book of the company or reinforce new rules. It is the mere fact that I am standing up for my rights. We are no longer living in the regime of slavery; therefore, I have the democratic right to fight back without fearing those who has become my opposition. Be that as it may, people sometimes push you and then they forget that you too can push back. I am going to push so hard for my name to be cleared.

However, this is a big step I am taking and I will show no pity because inside me is the willpower to bring about change, and I am not taking it lightly. I am nobody's saviour.

I am just disputing my injustice. This is my contribution to humanitarian intervention to fight those who impose harmful strategies to people who work hard to make a living.

I sometimes think and have seen it that when you reach a certain age, the top dogs of the company will find a way to get rid of you so that a younger person can replace the older version. Very little is done to prevent these kind of situations and it is seldom seen. So now is the time to break the cycle of this abuse and the power of the oppressors who continually play by their own rules. Again, it is only my analytical way of putting it together and I could be wrong with my analysis. The fact is, I am a woman in trouble and one can come up with many ways of thinking to find a solution.

Financially, I am in no position to sustain myself but I am waiting anyhow for the outcome of the case. So whichever way, I still have to wait for the outcome of the case; therefore, I work on this project to voice my opinion and to expose the abusers of my fate. This is not revenge. This is a wake-up call to put a stop to the ruthless men and women in authority that continually make it their duty to withhold the growth of the working class trying to make a living. Someone must retaliate; someone must be prepared to say 'This is wrong'. I might lose everything I worked for but I will not allow my freedom of fighting for my rights to be chained. Be that as it may, this is my platform to use my voice.

Anyway, I waited to be reinstated but I received no phone call and no letter. Nevertheless, I started feeling the strain of my unpaid house and was starting to stress. Warning letters were flowing in from the bank, and time and again, I read threatening messages on my mobile phone. I was swimming in debt now – piled-up arrears.

Standing in my kitchen and looking at my beautiful mahogany building cupboards that I worked so hard to pay for, thinking how I was going to lose this house I worked for and paid with my sweat, hard-earned money, and I was going to lose it all. It made me hate my superiors and the bank even more. What happened to me had started to change my character. Walking to the lounge my eye caught a book that was lying on the television unit. The book belonged to my sister. With a cup of tea in my hand I carefully picked it up and read the heading on the cover: *Love your life* by Victoria Osteen. I quickly placed the book back because I felt that the timing was wrong for me to love my life now. Nowadays, tears simply dropped unannounced from my eyes and I can assure you it is not tears of joy. The emotional pain comes from a deep place.

However, God always sends some help, a Good Samaritan, and he sent me that helping hand. Was the statement of Uncle John manifesting 'Cast your bread upon the water?' Without asking, my Samaritan called one afternoon and told me to come around to collect the money to settle the arrears of my bond. I cried that day and realised how much my Maker loves me. At least it would hold back the bank not to auction my house. At least for a few months I would be out of the red. It would give me a bit of time. Yes, time could sometimes become our worst enemy. As for now I respected the bit of time I was given as I waited for the outcome.

Many weeks went by, and I felt how my body was taking a toll with the fatigue of stress. I waited for a letter or a call from the post office but received no letter and no call. There were days I felt lost and helpless but I dragged myself to remain positive. I tried hard to be strong but it was hard to be strong under those circumstances. Every day I felt the sorrow of being subjected to a miscarriage of justice. I was in a mental prison of fear but I could not allow myself to be drowned in this sorrow. I needed to stay focused and pursue persistently.

All these emotions made me look older yet wiser, and sometimes I simply felt like throwing in the towel and call it a day, but my mind forced me not to quit. There were times that I was so broken and worried inside that the thoughts of suicide would come up. The inner struggle of my Christian belief would overpower those thoughts of suicide and I would just dismiss it from my mind and reroute them back into outer darkness. What I needed to remember was the vow I made to myself to fight back. I needed to be braver and bolder; it was not easy but I could try harder. This was a war and a painful one but I would have to bleed to survive for the sake of my children. No use to sit and mope being the emotional hostage of my own mind.

I must believe in my innocence because the truth will always set one free. I should become like a spitting cobra ready to strike, but I will wait upon the Lord to direct me in this fight. My future was in God's hands because I believed that he knew me before the beginning of my time and to worry so much would only make things worse. I worked hard to build and provide a security for my children and myself. The Bible says, 'In all labor there is profit'. I had laboured and no one had the right to take away my profit. By quoting the Bible, I needed to trust God and not lose hope. Through all these emotions of stress and betrayal I should show boldness when my kids are around so that I don't stress them out. Children are sensitive and sometimes adults think that the kids do not take note of everything. They might not ask many questions but they see and read one's body language. They know there are some troubles but I am sure that in their little minds they know Mama will handle it.

This whole nightmare made me closer to my Maker and I was reaching a spiritual realm. I was learning the hard way. I could never understand the saying 'When days are dark, friends are few'. Now I know what it meant. The few I had had suddenly become very busy and very scarce. Their mobile phones went on voicemail, and yes, this is life. Families were not interested to get involved, and they had their own lives. I understood that because this problem was mine and mine alone. However, with the few friends and family who cared for us – we were coping just fine. Life is hard for now but God is good. Every beginning has an end and the day will come when I will be on my feet again. Now it is my battle and I dare myself to be ferocious in it.

Anyway, there was a time I wanted to change my cellular number because of random people calling me but not to encourage me. You get the so-called friend who would call just to ask if there was at least food in my house because they were just back from Nando's chicken outlet. Other callers would ask me if I was still in my house, or was it repossessed. One day I overheard how some people were exchanging jokes about my situation. I was the joke while the fire of the spirits in the alcohol they were drinking was slowly intoxicating them. The fighting spirit within me was growing fiercely to fight the course. Their words did not kill the fighting spirit within me. However, what they did not know was that I would only be the victim of the jokers on a temporary basis. Could people be crueller than this? These are the people who had the ability to break my spirit down and invade my privacy and I decided not to take their calls anymore. Nevertheless, I tried hard not to expose my suffering, with the result I sold more beauty products and it helped me with a few rand to at least buy food and spending money for the kids. I worked on a tight budget and the kids learnt to accept whatever there was on their plates to eat. My children were adapting to the new because in their hearts they understood.

It was so agonizing for me to see that I was bent on changing my world because I was paying for the wrong of someone else. I paid for this transgression with my future and my tears. My life was dedicated to the Corporate Z, and production and profit were my code words. So what happened to the 'non-racial and equal, supposed to be just' society? What just society? My duty was towards my work at the Corporate Z which I cherished with my life. Recalling the heroic struggles, my time, and my presence that I gave with love – love for my work. I remember the days with the MTN and Sasol shares when people could buy shares from mega companies. Many flogged to the Corporate Z to buy shares and we would be so busy that I could not even take lunch. Sometimes the takings of the day would be more than a million rand and now I was being accused for stealing R42,250. I could be called anything, but not a thief. As a branch manager I tried hard and most of the staff would work with me as a team to stay within the budget. We tried hard to save the company money and hated wasting little items like the refreshments that were provided for the staff. I proudly can say that I have served the Corporate Z with distinction. Now I was faced with unemployment and answers for the prying ears and eyes. Those that make it their business to know about mine and get a kick out of it as if they are immune to mishaps. I am aware how people laugh behind my back and call me names, but one thing is for sure – they will never have the guts to say it to my face. I think of it as big barks from small dogs. It is sad when people put a profile together and think that they have windows to your soul – silly hackers. They may laugh now but my joy will come again. As for my situation, it had become the forerunner of my stress. It is common sense that stress is an evil that should never be allowed to flourish. The fact of the matter was no matter how hard I tried, stress was, in no uncertain terms, a perpetrator that lurked in my mind. With the result, I was struggling against an anger that beat me up.

Oh yes, it is a hard time for me. Moments of depression and on my own I have to cope with these adverse circumstances. Nevertheless, my choice is to endure – sometimes in despair but eager to pursue. My life is extremely complicated but I will not be controlled by all these complexities. What I need to do now is to guard against all bitterness that will only lead me to greater regrets because sometimes I do feel a malignant feeling. I must stay fortified by the principle of my beliefs and not rule out the beauty of life completely out of my mind due to this one mishap.

It was now the middle of June 2012 and I was still waiting for the Corporate Z to give me answers. Then I called Lucky (she had a similar case but with another branch) and she and I decided to go to the Department of Labour to find out how far our cases were. Our files were not there because the legal department has booked it out for review and we needed to make an appointment with them. The lawyer contacted me and told me that my case was very strong and that he would defend me in the Labour Court but that I would have to wait for a date because the courts were in recess until the end of July. He spoke to me at length explaining the dynamics of the case to me. I was also told that they had offered a settlement of six months' salary and my pension but no reinstatement. The lawyer said he had refused it for the simple reason that it was unfair and because my pension fund was legally mine. I had worked for it and it was not negotiable. I felt much better after the lawyer spoke to me and my hopes were high again as I was patiently waiting for the date of the case. Now it all depended on the person who was going to represent me, the findings of the Labour Court, and time. In all due fairness the deponents filing affidavit on behalf of the Corporate Z to depose the ruling of the Commissioner was beyond me.

While being alone most of the time, I sit down and reflect on many things. I watch the news and it depresses me even more. Life is full of unrest. The chaos is growing day by day. I feel that we all should take out some time away from all the madness and uncertainty and just breathe. We all need a break from this rat race. The human race does not know how to reflect on joy anymore. We are all so taken up with the problems of the world that we forget how to enjoy ourselves. There is indeed a time for everything and time never stops us to enjoy the gift of life – our circumstances do. We don't know what it is like to be calm and relaxed. Harmony is replaced by stress and laughter is replaced with sobs. Everyone fears because no one knows what the future holds. Right now I fear and I hide behind my fear. However, this fear had a beginning and this beginning will have an end – I could not imagine otherwise.

Life in this world is becoming scary. Most of us have built up self-defence strategies because we look at the world as a battlefield. We have to fight for everything. We fight for a seat in the taxi, dispute and disagree with schoolteachers, and have disagreements with family and our positions at work. It has become the order of the day to be on this battlefield. A battlefield where you question price increases of food, gas, school fees, utilities, and many more. We defend our properties, our children, and our business deals like how I am standing in defence of what has happened to me. Needless to say, the list is long and I now see that we are merely but pilgrims passing through in a world of unrest. It is because of my situation now, that I can see what is really going on. If I had been at work I wouldn't have seen it. No, I would have been busy with duties and that would have kept me focused. When we are in a comfort zone nothing else matters. Now that I am faced with a problem now I am able to see. It is a case of 'Once I was blind but now I can see'. Reality has stepped in because I too am left out in the cold and this kind of cold is what opens the eyes. My eyes can see what was invisible when things were okay with me. I had a job, food to eat, and money to buy whatever I needed and all was well and in place. What goes on in the world and in life was not my parcel because I was living my life and I had a life. But now that I am in distress, I see and know when it rains, it storms.

Our minds have been diverted to see what we see and how we see. No time to see any beauty in this world anymore. No time to observe nature and reflect on the natural beauty that has been given by the Creator. We have all become so busy and working so hard on new defence strategies that the little things in life have become nil and void in a world unknown.

It appears that the war has arrived and we are here to bleed. Yes, the battle is on. I say it because I know it – Why, because

I am bleeding. To say that the state of the world is sick will be a harsh understatement in the sense that we are missing the picture. It is true that my Broken Face is scared but I am not blind. It is highly inaccessible for me to think I have the answers. I answer my own questions and give myself the answers that I don't want to hear. But those who broke my face should never dare to think that they might lay claim to the entitlement of my life. Those deeds are in the hands of the Almighty. Because my life is in the hands of God and I know I have a purpose on this earth. Therefore, I will not stand to a decision already made by others concerning my future. Do I fear? Yes, I fear . . . I am terrified but the fear is what keeps me going and I press on to the mark to win this race. Can I persevere? Yes, I can, because I am going to. Of course it sounds arrogant, but I dare not collapse and die because I have children who need a mother to nurture and love them.

Anyway, one day I cleaned all my draws to get rid of all clutter not needed. I then came across old letters and documents. I carefully read through them to see which ones I could discard. One letter from the bank caught my eye and I could not help but laugh out aloud. In life money is not the ultimate but without it you cannot do what is needed. The worst part is that you don't count when you have no money – money talks. Nonetheless, in this letter the bank had notified me that I qualified for a loan of R300,000 which was a huge amount in that time period. The wording they used in the letter was very respectful. Amazingly, now that I am in trouble the wording in their letters has changed to threats. Yes, I am out of money and unemployed and now the whole situation changes. This is the name of the game. Money gives you strength, a voice, and respect. Without it, I repeat, without money we don't count. In any case, life goes on and one just has to be in that race and live. Anyway, I sell more beauty product to help my finances. Maggas, my friend, and my extended family buys from me and every cent I make helps to at least pay for something needed.

Yes, life goes on and can sometimes take a detour or just a different route. Fate is not something that can be stopped – we fall in love and we fall out of love. We see fortune and we experience misfortunes but it's life. I experienced one of those routes lately. I met up with a childhood friend and it wasn't long before we fell in love. Love had betrayed me twice but I was willing to give it another try. This guy was a widower and I was single. He had a daughter and I had two, so we gave our relationship a try.

The relationship with him was at least taking the focus away from my predicament. We would go out visiting or take our kids for excursions. All this was a more pleasant route for a change. This man made me see the beauty of life again. I found myself laughing instead of crying all the time. Through all these dark months there were good moments too. I took the kids on certain weekends and then we slept over at my friend's place in Bassonia. However, these people regard me as family and I am at home with them. We have a long-standing history; therefore I call them my extended family. Aunty Rose is always around to talk about the days when I was still a child. I grew up in front of her; she was our neighbour and I basically grew up in her house. This old lady is like a second mother to me and she and my mom are still close friends for many years. She will sit with my kids and tell them all about my childhood. How I helped in the soup kitchen. My new boyfriend also grew up in the same area and Aunt Rose knows his whole family history so his child also gets all the stories from her. In those days communities were close to each other. It was the apartheid regime and there were difficult times. We were living in a society where gangsters caused havoc in the townships. Our elderly knew that every child should be protected. Those were the days where one would say, 'I am my brother's keeper'. Children knew their place and adults were never disrespected. Youngsters who started to smoke would not even dare to do it when adults were around. Those were hard times but respectable because children were obedient. Nowadays, parents have become obedient towards their children.

Nevertheless, the kids enjoy it when we visit our extended family in Bassonia, because they like all the stories they hear from Aunt Rose, and so do I. Then there is Megan, my true friend – she will go out of her way to bring change and see me smile. Megan is always so concerned about me and for me that means that she is truly a friend. Then I also spend a lot of time with Maggas, my Brazilian friend. With Maggas there is never a dull moment; she can make me laugh the whole day and her accent is what makes it so amazing. Sometimes I get a Brazilian wax and my nails done because Maggas is a beautician. My mother sometimes takes the kids for a weekend so that I can enjoy a bit of 'me time'. As for my boyfriend, he never cramps my space and that is what I like about him. He knows when I need my time with the friends who really care and would never hold me back.

So all is not lost and I believe with all this support from dear friends and family I will heal and walk with pride again. It is funny that when we live our lives we never make provision for the turns that brings about disruption. Then the day when it strikes we just feel like life is over. Nevertheless, with the great people I surround myself with I dare not feel that my life is over. My honest friends teach me to take time off amid the problematic occurrences and treat me with love and patience. My heart I believe is in for repairs and soon it will be fixed but in the meantime I try hard to take a step back from the strain of life. This new unfortunate turn of events is a part of my history that I will soon conquer. Every moment in our lives is a part of our history. I learn every day how to protect myself from the hard words of others. Sometimes I have to hear from others about the talks going around about me being a thief. These are some of the hurdles I have to come across daily and fight. Be that as it may, our hurdles in life are there to teach us and to make us strong.

Every crisis tames me and helps me with all imperfections. Maybe it is a test to test my own loyalty to myself, I don't know. With all this said, what I do know? One thing is for sure; my Broken Face will heal and I will be alive and still standing to see my daughters for whom I worked for all my life – graduate. Never underestimate the perseverance of a single mother. I am engaged to my faith with my Maker so when I get challenged I will fight until I win. Maybe if I didn't have siblings, I would have called it a day and walked away just like a loser. But in this case, there is no way that it will happen – like I said, 'The perseverance of a single mother will prevail'.

To endure emotional strain is something I would not want to wish on anybody, because it is a strenuous road of many thorns and steep hills. But it made me to step into my greatness and triggered the violent desire within to accomplish my goal. Sometimes I am in despair but always eager to pursue. Nevertheless, it would be wrong to evade the mere fact that I am innocent; it has nothing to do with ego.

For now should I have lain still and been quiet,
I should have slept: then had I been at rest.

Job 3:13

CHAPTER 6

From what I heard was that the supplementary affidavit was forwarded to the Labour Court whereby the Corporate Z deposed the finding of the Commissioner amplifying the grounds of review.

According to them because I left the door to the walk-in safe unlocked for the tellers to gain access to their lockers and other valuables, was something that should not have happened. Irrespective of the fact that, that was the sequence of operations but they were not happy with the arbitration award. Therefore they referred the case to the Labour Court.

It was also indicated that the Commissioner failed to take into account the following.

The Applicant: Corporate Z. The Respondent: Sandra

a) It was the fundamental duty of a branch manager to safeguard the Applicant's assets.
b) The door to the walk-in safe was to be locked at all times.
c) The Respondent was duty-bound to control the keys to the safe.
d) Insofar as the tellers wished to gain access to the safe the Respondent ought to have controlled access.
e) By keeping the door of the walk-in safe open the Respondent acted negligently.

The Commissioner had emphasised that I had not deviated from the norm regarding the daily operations in my position. Yet they claimed that the Commissioner overlooked that the unlocked door of the walk-in safe resulted in the loss of money.

Likewise, I too had to certify an affidavit to admit the allegations. Therefore I did admit in my affidavit that on 15 December I failed to hand over the cheques to the value of R61,114.86 over to the collectors.

During the hearings I had mentioned many times the reason for not handing the cheques over to the collectors and I had also spoken about the suspect, which they never even investigated, but as I said earlier on, my word was not taken into consideration. All they wanted to prove was that I was guilty, but they couldn't prove it.

Imagine that day when all this happened – the whole office was in a state of chaos. How could I even request the collectors of the bank to wait until the matter is resolved? The only thing I could do was to ask them to rather collect the cheques on the next day when things would be more settled. The next day all the cheques were accounted for and were banked.

Throughout my term of service as a branch manager I had never delayed in banking cheques – it happened because of unforeseen circumstances out of my control. As for the accusation of being negligent, that I will deny until the day I die because I served the Corporate Z with my sweat and blood.

In my affidavit I stated:

It is unfair for me to be penalised for pleading my innocence and to be dismissed on a mere suspicion when clearly guilty employees in the past have not been dismissed.

This was another story on its own and I had brought it up in the hearings. In all due fairness, the Commissioner did take it into consideration. It was highly unlikely that the actions of a criminal could be controlled. I was in no way reckless in my job – with my life maybe but not with my job. I never played with my children's income. I followed all the correct procedures of my routine and job descriptions. The keys of the safe were given to other people in my absence several times and to claim that I was the only one entrusted with the safe's key was also wrong. The key to the safe was a normal burglar door key, and hypothetically speaking, who could say that a duplicate wasn't made in my absence? Why I say this is because it all boils down to that key now. All employees had access to the safe in order to perform their duties. Even so, the Employer was aware of that because that was the sequence of daily operations. Now it looked like it was my entire fault. In many management meetings I suggested for cameras to be installed but nothing was done to mitigate safety. But that was the thing with meetings; in my opinion, I think most of the time these meetings are just a formality. We all get together to voice our opinions but at the end of the day your words hang in the cosmos because you are just a worker and not a shareholder. Come on, who is fooling whom? I have at all times safeguarded the applicant's assets. It is so obvious; that is why they kept me employed for twenty years. Not because they think of me as cute, no, they know I am trustworthy because for the twenty years in service there are no records of me ever doing anything clandestine. So to exemplify, my name is my name and I want no nonsense with my name. That is why I will continue to fight for my name. My accusers are working hard to take away all I have worked for, but my name will not be dragged through the mud. This I say for the mere fact that I am innocent and for now, a victim, the little lamb ready for the slaughter and justice to deny me. Given these facts, can anyone blame me for fighting for my name?

But thou, O Lord, art a shield for me; my glory,
and the lifter up of mine head.

Psalm 3:3

CHAPTER 7

It was August 2012 – the last thing that was on my mind, the one thing I never thought would happen to me again, happened. Despite all my problems one sort of got used to the fact that unexpected news can just pop up. Well, I was unprepared for what I had to find out.

I found out that I was pregnant. I was not sure if I should be disappointed, confused, or should simply scream or laugh. Wow! What is this now, a baby in this time of so much trouble in my life? I heard from acquaintances how some people were working hard to construct the outcome of my case as if they were attending hearings on my behalf. All the same I was sure that they were doing it in such a way as if they were going to get marks for it. Or better even, as if they were going to get paid for it. By now I was well aware of who my friends were and who my friendly enemies were.

The static talks of others did not concern me anymore. I had learnt the art of laughing it off because there were many other positive things I could concentrate on. Currently, it does offend when people put too much effort in finding out about other people's business and fail to concentrate on their own problems. To put it straightforwardly, no one is without problems and life is never absent from problems. We all just live out that which was predestined for us.

I can just imagine what others who were in my situation had to go through with the treatment from people with loose mouths. Can they kick me further then my knees? I don't think so because on my knees I pray. I can relate to them but whichever way, I will proudly walk in public with my head held high because I am an innocent victim and not a criminal. I am not banished from society and I am still a free human being and the reason for my fight is to rectify the wrong. I will not allow the people who put together a short synopsis about my life to stop my movement as a person. To put it firmly, we are done with apartheid.

Many days I would sit alone and thank God for being with me. My footsteps are guided by a supernatural power through these troubled times. I strongly think that this turmoil is to discipline me and really it does.

Anyway, when I told my extended family about my pregnancy, it was a big joke to them. They laughed while I stood in dire amazement. I was unaware that with good judgment I was already scrutinised but not one of them felt that it was their place to tell me. At any rate, we were jesting about it and again I was given the moral and financial support. I have friends and family that stood by me from the day trouble started in my life. Therefore, I know they will be there when the time comes for this baby to be born. I am so blessed that I don't even stress about the situation of the Corporate Z. I know I placed my problems in the hands of God and I am going to leave it there for him to sort it out for me. In the meantime I have to take care of the bundle of joy in my womb, so the challenge is taking another unexpected route. Again I say time says nothing yet everything.

My boyfriend was elated with the news of the baby. He couldn't stop smiling and wished for a baby boy. All I wanted was a healthy baby – boy or girl. Love had betrayed me once but this man was a different man and I was growing to love him nowadays with all my heart. As for my family they were in shock to hear about the baby but made peace with it. Many other acquaintances were surprised and some of them pulled me over hot coals as if I were going to ask them for money to help. I was already so used to people who could say things without thinking. Imagine telling me, 'Can one be in a predicament like you and still afford to bring a baby into this world?' Oh please, when will people ever learn to mind their own business? Why don't they concentrate on their own skeletons because who is without sin to point fingers at others? I for one, refuse to yield because what people say about me is not my business.

My ordeal has taught me to hear and not hear, to see and not see. I believe that no one made me, so I allow no one to break me anymore. No one's words will ever again imprison my mind. There is no purpose in making myself unhappy over what others say or think about me. If it is their prerogative to make me the talk of the *Township*, then so be it; then they should enjoy their moments. I sincerely hope that those who talk and laugh would never drink from my cup. Maybe that is the only happiness they have, so let them have the laughs. Let's say, there is no cure for ignorance.

There was a reason for this pregnancy and I knew I was going to enjoy this baby. I prepared my two girls for the new life that would enter our lives and they too embraced the news with joy. My firstborn said to me maybe having this baby was what I needed. Yes, no baby could be a mistake. God never makes mistakes, and maybe this was to teach me something much better in life.

Since I was pregnant I enjoyed more pampering from my extended family. Maggas was very excited because she insisted that I would have to do the Brazilian wax now for the birth. I only laughed it off because she knew waxing was not my forte. The last time she waxed me she told me I was a real crybaby and I screamed like a pig that was ready for slaughter. I would rather stick to the old-fashioned way and shave.

Together my daughters and I went and looked for baby clothes and we tried to guess if it would be a boy or a girl. At night we sat on my bed and we talked about names for the baby. The three of us were so excited and seeing my girls so happy made a huge difference. I read their body language and saw the excitement in their eyes when they talked about helping with feeding, bathtime, and making baby go to sleep. This news of the baby brought us closer. I got tea on time, my feet got rubbed, and my girls tried their utmost best not to upset me. How blessed could I be and what was I going to do without my little girls? They added so much value to my life.

My first visit to the clinic for check-up took my mind far. This time the pregnancy was different from the previous ones. No medical aid, so no private gynaecologist. This baby would be born in a government hospital and not in a private hospital. Again my mind went to the fact how money talked and worked for you when you had it. Yes, God was showing me how the simplicities of life could do the same function. The poor has no access to the fast medical care. Here at the government clinic no matter who you are, you will get up early in the morning to stand in the queue. You will wait for your turn to get attended when the nurse calls out your number. It has nothing to do with an appointment that you have made. It is about first come, first served; you will wait for your turn – period.

At the government hospital things work differently. No special treatment for certain people. Everybody gets the same treatment. I observed everything and I enjoyed myself. It was like being in primary school. The nurse lectured all expecting mothers.

'Ladies, always make sure your feet are clean. We don't want you to lay in maternity with your legs in the air and dirty feet as a view. And please bring your own toiletries and do not forget a brush and a comb.' It sounded so funny but she was serious and authoritatively continued.

'Ladies, after you gave birth let not these little ones get a fright when they see your hair standing like a bush ready to be burned when we bring them for their first breastfeed. Really, we want all babies to experience love at first sight and not fear at first bite.' This was what I missed out with my other pregnancies. No one here tried to be diplomatic. The nurses were straightforward and very comical and I liked the atmosphere. So with great happiness in my heart I was ready for the new twist in my journey.

¹The Lord is my shepherd; I shall not want.

² He maketh me to lie down in green pastures: he
leadeth me beside the still waters.

³ He restoreth my soul: he leadeth me in the
paths of righteousness for his name's sake.

⁴ Yea, though I walk through the valley of the
shadow of death, I will fear no evil: for thou art
with me; thy rod and thy staff they comfort me.

⁵ Thou preparest a table before me in the
presence of mine enemies: thou anointest my
head with oil; my cup runneth over.

⁶ Surely goodness and mercy shall follow me all
the days of my life: and I will dwell in the house
of the Lord for ever.

Psalm 23

CHAPTER 8

It hurts me to think that I must go through another festive season where I cannot provide for my children and give them what they deserve. They brought home such good reports and have even received diplomas and awards, yet I have nothing else to give them but my love. I know that they understand the situation but as a mother and their only provider, I feel terrible. Through all my troubles I am with many people who care about my well-being. Our extended family in Bassonia has invited us for the holidays and I know we will enjoy our festive season.

Christmas Eve of 2012 was a highlight in my life. I was in Bassonia visiting my extended family and all the people who love me were there. Jailma, our sister-girl from Cape Verde, prepared snacks and Janice was just back from New York. Maggas couldn't make it because she was fully booked with last-minute clients who needed grooming for Christmas and New Year. At twelve that night we all exchanged presents – it was a real family gathering. Xee and Zasha could not stop taking photos with their Nikon cameras. This night was all about happiness and love. When one experiences so much love you just can't think of stress. In my eyes I had tears of joy. In the kitchen we all helped Aunt Rose with the Christmas preparations. Doing this all together in one kitchen was really like sisters coming together to bond. The next day we all enjoyed our Christmas lunch and later all the youngsters went out to hook up with their friends. This was one feast that will always stay fresh in my mind. Good moments like these will never fade from my life and truly such moments make me love my Broken Face.

Nobody can come up against me with this metaphor of Broken Face because it is mine. It talks about the invasion of my integrity, my sweat, my time, my reputation, and my life. Then it describes my perseverance, my battle, my disappointment, and my anger. Most of all, it speaks about the demonstration of my willingness to stand up for what is right, and last but not least, it sketches my emotions, my misfortune, my pain, and my endurance. Then in closure it summarises my instilled peace because this Broken Face is mine and it is the original. This Broken Face is daily teaching me about the sorrows of life and how I can conquer it through the consistency of believing in my innocence. This Broken Face has triggered the fighting spirit within me, and when the battle is over, I shall triumph and garnish the Broken Face with a smile to illustrate my natural elegance attained. Furthermore, I will enter into a new future and merge with it. It will be a new birth; then people will remember the woman with the Broken Face who stood up for her constitutional rights.

Beareth all things, believeth all things,
hopeth all things, endureth all things.

I Corinthians 13:7

CHAPTER 9

In January 2013 I decided to call my representative to ask about the case. I was provided with the information that the case was heard on 21 December 2012 and was reviewed in terms of Section 145 of the Labour Relations Act 66/1995 and they were awaiting the judgment. Again I had no other option but to wait. In the meantime life had to carry on.

As the months went by, all my loved ones started preparing for the arrival of my baby and I did what I needed to do. I went to the clinic for my check-ups, cleaned, cooked, and visited my mom and friends. I still heard the gossip stories and when I saw people they frowned and looked at me with a 'question mark'. I looked back and wondered if I should feel ashamed or guilty. But then I thought how stupid it was and would b the fool. When things go wrong in one's life then one lear who are the honest and genuine people one knows. The t

I have in my truth is divine and the words from the poisonous tongues of others are not my concern. Not only do I stand accused in my workplace but also judged by society. It has always been a human concern to worry and care what others say or think about us. When I am around old acquaintances I cannot but help question about the gossiping going on about me. Although I keep on telling myself I don't care what people say I still worry about the 'what if's and would try and hear from Megan or Joslyn. They are my true friends and know how to take my focus away from that topic.

At any rate, Megan and Joslyn organised a baby shower and many of my colleagues attended and showered me with gifts for the baby. A month before the expected date of the arrival of the baby I was surprised with a suitcase of baby clothes and accessories. I truly regard myself under all these adverse circumstances most richly blessed. Sometimes our circumstances remove the scales from our eyes for us to see the blessings in our complex lives.

Then came the long awaited call. On 7 March 2013 my superiors phoned to notify me to resume my position the next day. It was a most welcome news and yet I was not sure what to feel. I called up my extended family in Bassonia and they screamed with delight.

'It is finally over, baby,' Aunt Rose said over the phone in a trembling voice. 'I am crying tears of joy today, Sandra.'

I felt my own warm tears running down my face; yes, I broke down like a little child. When I was done with all my calls I went down on my knees to thank God.

This feeling was indescribable and I couldn't wait for my kids to come home so that I could share the good news with them. It was a joy beyond human explanation. I was trembling and crying; tears and snot was freely running down my face. I ran to the bathroom, looked in the mirror, and I saw my Broken Face wet with tears. I grabbed the toilet paper and rolled a big piece to blow out my nose. Then I washed my face with cold water and my gaze went back to the mirror. I calmly said a short prayer of thanks again because my Maker was with me until the end. After praying I opened my eyes and looked back into the mirror to take another look at my Broken Face, and what did I see? I saw triumph and the beauty of a completed goal. My tear ducts opened up again and I cried but it was fulfilling and therapeutic because this was the final anguish that came with tears of joy. No longer was I persona non grata. The Broken Face cried the tears of a winner and realised that she would no longer be under the constant surveillance of slandering tongues. Today I honoured the creative power within me for the willingness to persevere when I could have walked away and suffered defeat caused by my own silence, the unwillingness to stand up in defence. But here I stood crying tears of victory.

By the time my children came from school I was calm and my food pots were on the stove. This day was just different because they were greeted with an atmosphere they had not seen for a long time. Hearing the good news their little faces revealed expressions of excitement and I could only imagine what went through their childish minds because they had sacrificed with me.

My daughters knew everything about my dismissal be I had explained it to them. I had to conceal my tea that day when I explained how my dismissal would affect our livelihood. However, I assured them not to worry because the situation would be sorted out.

Some people would think it cruel but I needed to tell them so that they would understand the change. It was only fair not to deceive my children because people talk and they might hear it from another source. No more spending and shopping sprees like before and eat what there was to eat without complaining. Being an open book to them was helping them and me. It had disciplined them so much to appreciate everything we had. They didn't ask too many questions; they just knew that somehow it would be resolved. They had had enough trust in their breadwinner.

That night the girls helped me to put an outfit together for my first working day.

'Do they know that you are pregnant, Mom?' Agatha asked me.

'A few of them know but it will be a nice surprise for those who don't,' I answered calmly.

'But won't you be in trouble again?' she said with concern and I noticed the fear in my daughter's eyes.

I took her in my arms and said, 'My baby, we are done with trouble,' and I gently pulled her closer for a motherly hug. The type of hug that made her feel safe and in addition a promise at it would all be okay. Seeing the worry in my child I now despised the obstacle my children had to go through. realised how all this time of struggle, waiting and had affected them. Need I say that this Broken Face shall as from tomorrow be back in that office transformed and be ready for better days? I shall in no uncertain terms claim back what is rightfully mine. I will nowadays work hard to preserve my children from a cold world. However, it is not the world that is cold but people. My ordeal will never change my characteristics of being a person with a good heart; no, I will always be polite to my fellow men and treat them with respect.

Together the girls and I kneeled at my bedside and we prayed in all humbleness for God to prepare for the day.

To the praise of the glory of his grace, wherein
he hath made us accepted in the beloved.

Ephesians 1:6

CHAPTER 10

My first day at work was a day of great animated joy. The sudden diversion of my life turned from abnormal to normal – how bizarre. The woman with the Broken Face walks in and it was as if I was stepping on air because every step I took was with evident confidence – I claimed the floor I was walking on and the floor received every step with honour. The furniture praised me. I felt that even the walls were welcoming me back. Heads were raised, mouths stood open, and I was gazed at with peering eyes. Prying eyes looking for intimate details. I raised a brow but smiled to express my approval for their curious question marks. What spiced it up was that I was in my last stage of pregnancy. This was it – the countdown of my victory and it felt good. I felt fearless and alive and the masterpiece of my disaster would turn into the perfectness of my future. Walking the way I now is like a merit of a thousand victories. I deserve to this way because I cried more than a thousand times. So now that I have earned my victory, I return back to my life with no disgrace on my Broken Face, left with scars as a token of the memory of my pain. My truth was not meant to be buried but to set me free. The truth prevailed because truth conquers all.

This is the moment of truth and I am the owner who occupies this platform. With more determination and confidence I slowly walked one step after the other making a statement, not to anyone but to myself. With each foot landing on the floor, I proudly claimed back my dignity and headed to my sanctuary, my office. This is the final anguish and it comes with joy and the spirit of independence. I am in my office and I go for the chair – my chair, my office, and last but not least, my job. I felt ready to resume with my duties and to retain back my credibility.

Many people would think my fight was about revenge. I fought not only for a cause but also to survive and for my honour to be restored. With this new future I will encourage and inspire others and that to me is a perfect caption as I am going to deal with the present. Every moment in my life is a mystery and healing for my mind. No longer will poor sleeping patterns have an impact in my life. My sleep will be sweet because I have conceived a new life that I embrace with the knowledge that I will achieve my heart's desires.

Here I am back where I belong, the victim who now owns the victory. Once a sacrifice now I am liberated and I embrace it with cheerfulness. The truth has prevailed and I am a conqueror and that makes me an illustrious woman. The broken pieces I will put together again because my new existence starts from now. It is my right to take my life and privacy back and I will it with the passion of my achieved goal. One thing is for sure — I have made history and will be seen as the woman with the distinctive character. But from this day on, my kids and I will renew our once interrupted lives whereby I will implement a new protocol to love and protect them from all complexities with superfluous precaution. That is the invisible force that remains within me. With much confidence I can say that the dark days of struggle, waiting and stressing is weakened and the 'war' is over because I have succeeded in my undertaking. No cluttered worries or anxieties and best of all I am no longer the laughing stock of those who entertained themselves with my misfortune. To summarise, the bleeding process of this ordeal is over.

So with gentle gutsiness I shall work hard on forgiveness. Forgive everyone who has wronged me and everyone who mocked me. As for those who judged me, I shall earnestly pray for them to never go through what I had to endure because perseverance and endurance does not come easily. What happened was a life-skill seminar and I regard myself stronger. I am not who I used to be; I am an incredible warrior and a top-notch survivor, rooted and grounded in what I believe is correct and fair. Life is full of many surprises and my ordeal was an unexpected surprise. I have brought my story to light and I am at peace. It will take time to rebuild my life again but perseverance has taught me to never doubt myself. All I know is I fought not only for a cause but also to survive the odds. I am ready to go on to the next level no matter what anyone says. What people say or think about me is not my concern. I will not forget that it was I who lay awake at night while others were sleeping peacefully.

On 13 March I was rushed into hospital and gave birth to another baby girl. When I held her in my arms and looked at her pretty face I gave God the glory. My daughter Agatha was right; this baby was what I needed and here she lay in my arms. I felt proud that God had entrusted the precious life of this baby in my care and I accepted the responsibility to take good care of her and my other two. My newborn's father was also happy for his baby and on the third day we were allowed to go home. I am on maternity leave at the moment and life is taking a better turn for me. The new bundle of joy brings much delight to our lives and this time I have a man around who cares for his child. All the turmoil has prepared me for better days and much happiness. Without doubt, from now on I will not only create my destiny but also my atmosphere to enjoy the beauty of life.

Ye are bought with a price; be not ye
the servants of men.

I Corinthians 7:23

CHAPTER 11

I usher in a new future and a new life I conceived for my children and me. I will evoke the happy days and no longer see the immense toil on my Broken Face because it is going through its healing process. I embrace life with new hope. You see, this was a war, my war and my task. Sometimes we misjudge the devices of those with dishonest hearts then you fall prey to their devious works. Therefore, I will slowly withdraw into secret caution, my modified protocol of alertness and order. I feel free and it is what I was longing for. I no longer have to fight for my job — my focus is on my new baby. I will later study further because before I was dismissed I have completed a course in *Woman in Leadership* and I must admit that, that course also helped me to stand up for my rights.

Days are passing by and I spend enough time with my children to help them with schoolwork. I live according to my new rules which I have set for myself. I no longer have to struggle to wake up, feeling tired and scared to face a new day. Fear and worry cannot bluff me anymore because I have many beams of light in my life again. The struggle I endured has opened new mysteries. Insomuch that I will be able to inspire and encourage others and honour each day I live with gratefulness. No longer does poor sleeping patterns have an impact – my sleep is sweet. No self-doubt that reminds me of my fear that I would lose everything and go hungry. No achy joints and bodily pains. I declared war on pain that was caused by stress. All fears I challenged with shield and armour. It will take time and sacrifice to build my life to perfection but I am positive I will achieve that goal. I shall triumph when everything is in place and know that I am the one who leads by example. Out with the chains of conspiracy and the walls of its prison that has violated my life and put my future dreams on hold. My spirit was sick but now it is healed. Day by day I find fresh tranquillity and I treasure life because I have come to life and happiness embraces me. With great confidence I will enter into more of my greatness to receive more of what life has to offer.

Now I walk away with the *Nobel Prize*, knowing I have conquered. I am free of all charges and it is called *Not Guilty*. No matter the conditions that accompany a situation, from now on I will wake up knowing that life is a blessing. We all go through a dark tunnel of trouble in our lives at times but at the end of that tunnel there is an opening and through that opening there awaits light and fresh air. I was wronged but I will continue to be a forgiving person bearing in mind that my Maker forgives me every day of my life. It is not so much about winning but about the learning process one gets from the experience, a kind of wake-up call that nothing should ever be taken for granted. I learned that patience, perseverance, the understanding of how things work, and the reality of going with the flood of troubled waters are the moments that refines one's character. I am so grateful to all the people who helped me financially, mentally, and spiritually – I will forever remember their love for my children and me. I might come across as arrogant within the pages of this book but it was only my self-defence strategy I created at the time. Forgive me, for I am but human and to err is human. Please do listen up – I am still that humble, gentle, loving person because all is back to normal. Now I am at peace with myself and grateful that the error is rectified. I am grateful that I have my job back and grateful that I am a survivor. Yes, I have stepped into my greatness to possess the quality I have. In truth, such courtesy should never be taken away from anyone who dares to fight the odds. Braced with new visions to appreciate the beauty of wisdom and purpose of life I am out of the valley with new wings to fly away from all my yesterdays. On this planet no matter what the circumstances, there is grandeur and I honour the gift of life.

On 1 August 2013 I resumed my duty at Corporate Z and it was as if nothing ever happened. It is business as usual and with forceful authority I can proudly say my name because I fought for it with the shield of my human rights. Now I honour myself with a medal (this book), as the history of my legacy will remain. I have done my time and now I am in my time again. The truth is, we are all here to do our time – our time to exist in this life. I am Sandra, the woman who had the Broken Face, and I exist.

Quote from Sandra:

'Once upon a time when nothing was something, nowhere were somewhere, and someone was no one. For now it is: Something is nothing, somewhere is nowhere and the no one has become someone and went anywhere to everywhere. I am Sandra and I respect my healing face.'

Sandra

A good name is better than precious ointment;
and the day of death than the day of one's birth.

Ecclesiastes 7:1

EPILOGUE

Sandra told me that she now knows that it is imperative to depend on the three pillars of life, which are religion, politics, and finances. In addition to these pillars, there are the spiritual, physical, and mental emotions. According to her she was a single mother in crisis but the three pillars were standing strong. It was her belief in her Maker, her democratic rights, and the friends and families who supported her financially. She was not prepared for the unexpected turnabout in her life but has learned for the future never to fear disappointment. All changes she will learn to embrace and not go to war with herself. 'It is safe', she adds, 'to live above the line of my own thinking. I will never forget that I was sorely tested but with the help of all my heroes I had the strength to bear the burden. It has propelled me to a new life and a new mindset on a new journey.

'Time has approached infinity for me. Above all, can I question the set of terms? I made my contribution to the business world from the time I started to work. It was a question of priorities, and my work was always my priority. It is the painful battles we fight in life that brings out the best of who we really are. Then it tailors our characters, transforms our mental outlook, and expands our world. I made my choice to stand and fight like a warrior when the war arrived for me.

'Now I am free from the emancipation of the unruly occurrence and I can exhibit the energy that will take me back step by step into my new future. My emancipation I demanded because of the burden of shame I had to endure. My emancipation is indeed my new revolution. The difference is the journey of my *bleeding period* was a profound learning process that gave me enough courage to face any challenge that would come my way in the future. As for what I stood for was for the sake of my name and my children. How could I simply just resist the willingness to defend myself, call it quits, and feel lost and defeated? It was not only my basic human right but also my duty to help correct what was done to me in error. Although I might offend many with my undertakings, it was my constitutional right to stand up and be heard. In my understanding, it is only fair that I did what I needed to do. Nothing should deny anyone from the courtesy of the willingness to fight for what is right. Therefore, from the bottom of my heart I hereby thank the CCMA and the Labour Court for seeing my innocence and represented the findings in fairness. To all who helped me emotionally and financially I shall forever remember their compassion for my children and me. I bear no hatred within because the struggle of this journey made me humble, yet complete. Through it all I also had the privilege and gave love another chance. God gave me a new baby whom I named Tashnico and there is a reason why she has that name.

'I promised myself to have no further attachments with the dreadful situation once all is over. Needless to say, this truly was a critical situation but life goes on and I don't need to cringe anymore. I am back at work and happy in my position and really have no attachments with what happened. All I know is that I fought with all the strength that was within me. The truth conquered all and the truth has prevailed. Some painful dilemmas are better left in the past. It was a painful journey but I survived. My own experience with my emotions was not always very cheerful because I became sensitive to people's gossips. Now that it is all over I am in charge of my own thoughts and the holder of my vision. However, I believed in my innocence and God carried me through.

'The words of this book were written with tears and emotions. I fought long and hard for a course. Nevertheless, my tears have dried by themselves – tears of pain and joy. I have new dreams and a fresh zeal for life. All my painful yesterdays I leave in my past and each day I am looking forward to a new tomorrow. I am the original of who I am and I embrace my life with new hope. I cherish the future of being free from what happened because I believe that I am a symbol of perseverance. I served and stood out a punishment I did not deserve. Nevertheless, I am still standing strong. Being back at work is what matters – it is business as usual.'

Meet Me

Hello, everybody, remember me or don't you know me anymore?

Not that I care because really I don't; why, because you know what you do with me. Here you are without a clue of who I am, yet you know me. Forgetting that sometimes you love me and sometimes you don't. If I can just refresh your mind, there are times that you abuse and disrespect me. Then you lie to others and yourself – in my name. You play with me yet I am not interested what you do with me. You sometimes cry because you know you have lost me. Then you try to make up with me again, not that I mind. What you do with me does not concern me. I don't care about you and what you do because I am no respecter of person. I have no friends and I have no enemies. Who you are and what you have is not my concern. The games you play have no effect on me. What you feel for me is what you feel. You conduct deceit and lies in my name thinking that you are proficient in what you do. Only you are the mastermind of the games that you play in my name. You are the one amusing yourself with what you do when you disrespect me. I am always there for you but you think you can fool with me – you fool yourself. You waste your own life while I walk on by.

Tell me, do you remember me now? Who am I? The truth is you know me but now you don't. Okay, let me introduce myself again.

Hello, everybody, my name is Time – don't play with me.

Zuzu Alexi Cupido
The Warrior